Your Guide to Cook Homemade Hot Sauce

Delicious Hot Sauce Recipes for You to Make at Home!

BY: Valeria Ray

License Notes

Copyright © 2020 Valeria Ray All Rights Reserved

All rights to the content of this book are reserved by the Author without exception unless permission is given stating otherwise.

The Author have no claims as to the authenticity of the content and the Reader bears all responsibility and risk when following the content. The Author is not liable for any reparations, damages, accidents, injuries or other incidents occurring from the Reader following all or part of this publication.

Table of Contents

Introduction 6

    Traditional Hot Sauce 7

    Sriracha Sauce 9

    Green Hot Sauce 11

    Red Chili Sauce 13

    Szechuan Chili Hot Sauce 15

    Hot Pepita Sauce 18

    Hot Steak Sauce 20

    Flaming Jalapeno Hot Sauce 22

    Fatalii Hot Sauce 24

    Cilantro Hot Sauce 26

    Hot Pineapple Sauce 28

    Red Devil Hot Sauce 30

    Asian Spice Hot Sauce 32

    Spanish Chili Sauce 34

Garlic Hot Sauce 36

Tropical Hot Sauce 38

Iran Pepper Hot Sauce 40

Habanero Hot Delight Sauce 43

Whammo Hot Sauce 45

Fiery Ghost Surprise Hot Sauce 47

Twisted Hot Sauce 49

Mango Tango Hot Sauce 51

Bajan Hot Sauce 53

Quick Hot Pepper Sauce 55

Belizean Style Habanero Hot Sauce 57

Jamaican Hot Sauce 59

Buffalo Chipotle Hot Sauce 61

Scotch Bonnet Pepper Sauce 63

Chickasaw Hot Sauce 65

Chiltepin Hot Sauce 67

Conclusion 69

About the Author 70

Author's Afterthoughts 71

Introduction

If you're a hot sauce lover and have always wondered how to make hot sauce at home, wonder no more! This recipe book is here to help! Filled with appetizing and mouth-watering hot sauce recipes, this book will help you create the amazing hot sauce recipes that will impress everyone!

What's more, all the recipes in this book are simple and come with step-by-step instructions. Plus, the recipes can be easily doubled or tripled if you want! So, what are you waiting for? Choose a hot sauce recipe and let's begin!

Traditional Hot Sauce

Traditional red-hot sauce recipe.

Makes: 1 ½ cups

Prep: 5 mins

Cook: 15 mins

Ingredients:

- 2 tablespoons olive oil
- 1 large onion diced
- 2 medium chili peppers, use your favorite peppers, stems removed
- 3 habanero peppers, stems removed
- 4 garlic cloves, minced
- 1 lb. of tomatoes, diced
- 1 cup distilled white vinegar
- 2 teaspoons salt
- 2 teaspoons sugar

Directions:

Set your oil over medium heat.

Add the onion, peppers, habaneros and garlic, cook for 5 minutes, stirring occasionally.

Lower to medium heat and add tomatoes, vinegar, salt and sugar.

Cook, stirring occasionally, for 5 minutes.

Transfer to your food processor then process until smooth.

Strain the contents, using a fine mesh sieve, over a medium bowl and push out all the solids to extract all the liquid.

Toss the solids and allow your sauce cool to room temperature.

Sriracha Sauce

Learn how to make Siracha sauce at home with this simple recipe!

Makes: 16 oz.

Prep: 1 week to ferment

Cook: 10 mins

Ingredients:

- Red jalapeño peppers (1 ¾ lbs.) stems removed and halved lengthwise
- Garlic (3, cloves)
- Granulated sugar (3 tbsp.)
- Brown sugar (1 tbsp.)
- Salt (1 tbsp.)
- Vinegar (¾ cup)
- Water (½ cup)

Directions:

Put garlic and peppers along with sugar and salt into a food processor. Blend until a coarse texture is formed.

Put mixture into a glass jar and store in a dark place at room temperature for a week. Stir daily. (May show signs of fermentation)

Take the mixture after a week and pour into a saucepan along with vinegar and allow to boil over medium flame.

Lower heat and cook for five mins. Remove from flame and allow to cool.

Run mixture through processor adding water where necessary.

Strain finally mix and add additional seasoning if you desire.

Then pour into a glass jar, close and refrigerate.

Green Hot Sauce

This green hot sauce is perfect for curries.

Makes: 1 jar

Prep: 5 mins

Cook: -

Ingredients:

- 1 cup washed Cilantro, leaves
- 2 tbsp. water
- 1 tbsp. dry mango powder
- 1 big tomato, chopped roughly
- 1 big onion, chopped roughly
- ½ cup washed mint, leaves
- 5-6 green chilies or to taste
- 6-7 garlic cloves, peeled
- Salt to taste
- 1-inch piece of ginger, chopped roughly

Directions:

Blend all the ingredients in a blender.

Serve with Indian dishes, as a side dish or as a dip for snacks.

Store in refrigerator.

Red Chili Sauce

This delicious hot sauce is often enjoyed in Portugal, Brazil, and Africa.

Makes: 1 jar

Prep: 10 mins

Cook: -

Ingredients:

- 6 red chilies, remove stems, wash
- 4 garlic cloves, chopped
- ½ tsp. red chili flakes
- 6 tbsp. cilantro/parsley or both
- Juice of ½ a lemon
- ¼ cup olive oil
- Salt to taste

Directions:

Add your ingredients to a blender. Blend until you get a smooth consistency.

Transfer into a glass jar, then cover and refrigerate.

Szechuan Chili Hot Sauce

If you are seeking for a good hot sauce to be paired with fish dishes, this Szechuan Chili Hot Sauce has got you covered.

Makes: 4 cups

Prep: 20 mins

Cook: 15 mins

Ingredients:

- 1 cup of vegetable oil
- 6 tbsp. of green Szechuan peppercorns
- 4 star anise
- 1 black cardamom
- Green onions, 2 stalks, chopped into 1 inch pieces
- 10 cloves of garlic, peeled and smashed
- 4 tbsp. of red Szechuan peppercorns
- 1 stick of cinnamon
- 65 grams of chili flakes

Directions:

Take a small saucepot and place the saucepot over medium-high heat.

Add some vegetable oil to the saucepot.

Allow the vegetable oil to heat at 350 degrees Fahrenheit.

To check on whether the oil has heated enough, place a wooden spoon in the oil, just barely touching the oil and check if it will bubble at the edges.

Once the oil is hot enough, remove the saucepot from the burner.

Now, add all the other ingredients to the stockpot, while the oil is still very hot.

Gently stir the contents of the saucepot to mix and combine.

Set the stockpot aside to cool until the contents in the saucepot stop bubbling.

Once the contents are not bubbling any longer, cover the contents of the saucepot. Set to cool completely.

If possible, allow the contents of the stockpot to sit overnight.

Once completely cooled, sieve the contents of the saucepot using a wire mesh sieve.

Place the sieved contents in airtight sealed containers. Put the sealed containers in the refrigerator to store.

Hot Pepita Sauce

Combine the earthiness of roasted pumpkin seeds with a mixture of peppers to create this tasty Hot Pepita Sauce.

Makes: 1 jar

Prep: 10 mins

Cook: 20 mins

Ingredients:

- 1 cup pepitas (pumpkin seeds)
- ½ cup red wine vinegar
- ½ tsp. salt
- 2 tbsp. ancho chili powder
- ½ tsp. garlic powder
- ½ tbsp. olive oil
- ¼ tsp. cayenne pepper
- ½ tbsp. chipotle chili powder
- 1 ½ cups water

Directions:

Preheat the oven to 350F. Place pepitas in a baking dish and roast it in the oven until brown (20 minutes), stirring them once in a while.

Switch off your oven then place to cool for about 15 minutes.

Place the pepitas and all the other ingredients in a food processor.

Blend until smooth.

Pass through a sieve and transfer the sieved sauce into glass jars.

Cover and refrigerate.

Hot Steak Sauce

The Chocolate Bhut Jolokias in this recipe has a flavor that blends well with BBQ sauce.

Makes: 8 cups

Prep: 10 mins

Cook: 1 hr. 10 mins

Ingredients:

- Onion
- 1 ½ doz. Chocolate Bhut Jolokia chili peppers
- 2 Swiss Brown Mushrooms
- Lemon juice
- 1 ½ cup Apple Sauce
- 2/3 cup Mustard Seeds
- 2 tbsp. Mustard seed powder
- 2 tsp Curry Powder
- 2 tsp Sea Salt
- ½ cup Apple Cider Vinegar
- 1 tbsp. Cracked Pepper
- 4 cups BBQ Sauce

Directions:

Wash peppers and chop along with onions and mushrooms; place them separately in small bowls.

Cook onions and mushrooms in a pot over a low flame and then add mustard seeds. Add some vinegar to avoid burning and drying out.

Add the other ingredients and simmer for about an hour or until sauce has thickened.

Have right away with your choice of meat or bottle and refrigerate until needed.

Flaming Jalapeno Hot Sauce

Flaming is indeed the term to be used with this recipe. Get ready for a flaming burst of flavor from the jalapenos in this tasty sauce that can be paired with poultry or red meat.

Makes: 1 jar

Prep: 10 mins

Cook: 10 mins

Ingredients:

- 1 doz. jalapeno peppers
- 8 tbsps. Red wine vinegar
- 1 lime
- Sugar (1 tbsp.)
- Salt (½ tbsp.)
- Onion Powder (½ tbsp.)
- Garlic Powder (½ tbsp.)

Directions:

Firstly, wash the peppers then cut them in half and remove the seeds. Place them in a bowl. Put a pot with two cups of water to boil.

Pour on peppers in bowl and cover for a minute. Drain water from peppers and put them in a blender; squeeze lime onto peppers.

Then add vinegar, sugar, salt and onion and garlic powder and blend to mix ingredients together.

Pour mixture into a glass bottle & refrigerate. Use as you please with meals and enjoy.

Fatalii Hot Sauce

This is an easy fruity Fatalii Hot Sauce. Fatalii is great for the base for this sauce, the pears help thicken the sauce but do not overdo the fruity Fatalii. You can add lemon to this sauce, and it is perfect for seafood or chicken.

Makes: 8 cups

Prep: 10 mins

Cook: 1 hr. 15 mins

Ingredients:

- 2 cups Fatalii Chili peppers
- 3 cups Pears
- 1 cup White Wine Vinegar
- 1 stick Lemongrass
- Lemon juice
- 1 tsp Salt

Directions:

Wash peppers and remove their stems. Dice peppers and lemongrass and put them in a blender along with other ingredients except for salt.

Blend till liquefied and then pour into a pot and heat over a medium flame for about 15 minutes. Turn flame down to low and cook for an hour until reduced.

Add salt after the sauce has been reduced. Pour into sterilize bottles and refrigerate.

Cilantro Hot Sauce

Here we have another recipe that works well with seafood.

Makes: 1 jar

Prep: 10 mins

Cook: -

Ingredients:

- 1 cup hot chili peppers, sliced
- 2 cilantros, sliced
- 1 tsp. white sesame seeds
- 1 tsp. black sesame seeds
- 2 shallots, sliced
- 2 tbsp. peanuts, crushed
- 1 tbsp. garlic. Minced
- 2 tbsp. Sriracha sauce
- ¼ cup fresh cilantro
- 1 cup boiling water
- ½ cup seasoned rice vinegar
- 1 tsp. salt
- ½ tsp. sugar

Directions:

Add sugar and salt into a cup of hot water. Mix well until dissolved.

Add vinegar and whisk again. Place it in the refrigerator to cool.

To serve, mix together all the ingredients and add the vinegar solution.

Hot Pineapple Sauce

This recipe carries a rich, fruity flavor while still maintaining its spicy characteristics.

Makes: 1 jar

Prep: 10 mins

Cook: 10 mins

Ingredients:

- 6 Thai chilies (Bird's eye chili)
- 2 Habanero chilies
- ½ cup grated carrot
- Zest of ½ a lemon
- Juice of ½ a lemon
- ½ cup onions, chopped roughly
- 5 ounces Pineapple puree
- ¼ cup white vinegar
- ¼ cup sugar
- ½ tsp. salt

Directions:

Combine your Pineapple puree, onions, lemon juice, lemon zest, habaneros and chilies in a saucepan on medium heat.

Add in your salt and sugar then set to cook for about 10 minutes.

Cool slightly then transfer into a blender. Process until smooth then and in your vinegar. Blend to combine then bottle.

Keep covered and refrigerate.

Red Devil Hot Sauce

This delicious sauce got his name from being said to be as hot as the flames from down under.

Makes: 1 jar

Prep: 5 mins

Cook: 5 mins

Ingredients:

- 10 fresh habaneros, sliced
- 8 scotch bonnet peppers, chopped with seeds.
- 2 garlic cloves, minced
- 1 small onion, minced
- ½ tsp. vegetable oil
- ½ tsp. salt
- 125 ml cider vinegar

Directions:

Set your oil in a frying pan on medium heat.

Add onion, garlic, chili and salt. Sauté for 3-4 minutes.

Remove from heat. Cool.

Transfer into a food processor & blend with the cider until smooth.

Transfer into glass jars and store in refrigerator. This sauce lasts for 6 months.

Asian Spice Hot Sauce

This Asian Spice Hot Sauce is a strong peppery mix that is perfect for curries and stews.

Makes: 1 jar

Prep: 10 mins

Cook: 10 mins

Ingredients:

- 3 stalks of lemon grass, with the bottom part of the stalk sliced into small pieces.
- About 2-inch fresh turmeric root. Peel the turmeric and then chop into small pieces.
- 10 dried chilies
- 1 inch fermented shrimp paste.
- About 2 inch of galangal spice, peeled and then chopped fine into pieces.
- 12 candlenuts, crushed with a knife
- 3 cloves of garlic, peeled
- 20 shallots, peel the shallots and then cut into 2
- 3 tbsp. of vegetable oil

Directions:

Add all the ingredients apart from the vegetable oil to a blender.

Turn on the blender and blend until a smooth paste is formed.

Once the paste is formed and smooth, take a skillet and place the skillet over low heat.

Add some vegetable oil to the skillet and allow the oil to heat slightly.

Once the oil is heated, add the blended paste to the skillet.

Cook the paste while continually stirring to avoid sticking on the skillet.

Allow the contents of the skillet to cook until fragrant.

Once the paste is fragrant, remove the skillet from the burner.

Set the skillet aside to cool completely.

Place the paste in airtight jars and put in the refrigerator for up to one month, if not using immediately.

Spanish Chili Sauce

If you love extremely hot sauces, this Spanish Chili Sauce is for you.

Makes: 1 jar

Prep: 5 mins

Cook: 10 mins

Ingredients:

- 3 Spanish chilies, stem removed and seeded small red pepper, diced
- 1 can (14 ounce) whole tomatoes, pureed
- 1 small onion, diced garlic cloves, cut in half
- 1 tbsp. cider vinegar
- ½ tbsp. organic sugar

Directions:

Add all the ingredients in a pan & bring it to a boil.

Switch to low heat then simmer until the ingredients have turned soft.

Remove from heat and cool.

Transfer to your blender then blend until smooth.

Transfer into glass jars & refrigerate.

Garlic Hot Sauce

Garlic Hot Sauce is the perfect addition of spice to stir fry dishes.

Makes: 1 jar

Prep: 5 mins

Cook: 10 mins

Ingredients:

- Rice vinegar, 4 tbsp.
- Sugar, 4 tbsp.
- Light soy sauce, 2 tbsp.
- Soy sauce, 2 tbsp., dark
- Chili sauce, 1 tsp.
- Sesame oil, ½ tsp.
- Corn starch, 3 tsp.
- Water, 2 tbsp.
- Vegetable oil, 1 tbsp.
- Garlic, 3 tbsp., chopped finely

Directions:

Heat vegetable oil in a medium saucepan. Add garlic and sauté for about ½ a minute.

Add sesame oil, chili sauce, soy sauces, sugar and rice vinegar. Stir well.

Combine your water and corn starch in a bowl. Add it into the saucepan stirring constantly.

Bring to a boil. The sauce would have thickened. Use as needed.

Tropical Hot Sauce

This Tropical Hot Sauce is very hot so, be wary of the amount that you take on each bite.

Makes: 1 jar

Prep: 5 mins

Cook: 10 mins

Ingredients:

- 2 cups fresh pineapple, remove skin, chopped into chunks
- 2 ripe mangoes, peeled, chopped into chunks
- 4 scotch bonnet peppers, roughly chopped
- 1 cup water
- Juice of 2 lemons
- 2 tbsp. brown sugar
- ½ tsp. allspice
- ½ tsp. ground cloves
- 1 tsp. salt
- 4 tbsp. cider vinegar

Directions:

Place the mango, pineapple and peppers in a food processor and blend until you get a smooth consistency.

Transfer into a saucepan. Add rest of the ingredients. Simmer for 5-7 minutes.

Taste and adjust seasonings if needed.

Pass the sauce through a sieve by pressing it with a wooden ladle.

Transfer the sauce into glass jars. Cover and refrigerate.

Can last for a month.

Iran Pepper Hot Sauce

This tasty Iran Hot Sauce can be used as a spicy substitute for chimichurri.

Makes: 3 cups

Prep: 15 mins

Cook: -

Ingredients:

- 4 cloves of garlic, grated
- 1 lime
- 1 tsp. of cumin, ground
- ½ tsp. of pepper
- 3 bunches of fresh saffron, washed and dried
- 8 small Iran red peppers, remove the stems
- 1 tsp. of cardamom, ground
- 1 tsp. of salt
- ½ cup of olive oil

Directions:

Add the saffron to the bowl of a food processor.

Turn on the processor and process at low speed to shred the saffron.

Next, add the juice of one lime. Also, add some olive oil.

Now, pulse the contents of the food processor to form a paste.

Next, add the garlic. Pulse the contents of the food processor to mix and combine well.

Now, add the red chilies to the contents of the bowl.

Again, pulse the contents of the bowl until well incorporated.

Now, add the cardamom. Also, add some salt to season.

Now, add the pepper. Next, add the cumin.

Process the contents of the food processor until smooth and well mixed and combined.

You can then place the zhug, in an airtight container and put the container in the refrigerator for up to 3 weeks.

You could also place the container in the freezer for up to 6 months.

Habanero Hot Delight Sauce

This sauce is made with one of the hottest peppers in the world, so take special care to modify the recipe as you like.

Makes: 16 oz.

Prep: 10 mins

Cook: -

Ingredients:

- 1 doz. habanero peppers
- Carrots (2)
- Onion
- Garlic (6 cloves)
- Salt (½ tbsp.)
- White pepper (¼ tbsp.)
- Lime
- White vinegar (8 tbsp.)

Directions:

Firstly, wash the peppers then cut them in half and remove the seeds. Place them in a bowl. Put a pot with two cups of water to boil.

Pour on peppers in bowl and cover for a minute. Drain water from peppers and put them in a blender, squeeze lime onto peppers.

Then add onion, garlic, salt, white pepper and vinegar; blend to mix ingredients together.

Pour into a glass jar and refrigerate. Use as you please with meals and enjoy.

Goes well with pizza, hamburgers or chili and soup.

Whammo Hot Sauce

This sauce will put a "whammy" on you. Its sweet taste will pamper your taste buds and then "wham" the heat is on.

Makes: 16 oz.

Prep: 10 mins

Cook: -

Ingredients:

- Tomatoes (1 qt. can)
- Chili peppers (1 ½ cups)
- Onion (½)
- Sugar (1 cup)
- Vinegar (2 cups)
- Pickling Spice (1 tbsp.)

Directions:

Put pickling spice in a cheesecloth and tie. In a saucepan, put vegetables and vinegar along with spices and allow to cook until vegetables are soft. Remove from heat and strain and return to pan.

Add sugar and cook until it thickens to your liking, stir regularly to avoid sticking. Pour into clean glass jar(s) and refrigerate until needed.

Fiery Ghost Surprise Hot Sauce

Be warned that this sauce is not for amateurs. If you aren't on the extreme side of the spicy scale, then brace yourself.

Makes: 16 oz.

Prep: 10 mins

Cook: -

Ingredients:

- Ghost Peppers (3)
- Garlic (5 cloves)
- Onion
- Salt (½ tbsp.)
- White Pepper (¼ tbsp.)
- Carrots (4)
- Apple Cider vinegar (½ cup)
- Water (½ cup)

Directions:

First, wash ghost peppers then put them in a food processor. Add onion carrots and garlic and chop to combine.

Then add salt and white pepper to mixture. Add water and vinegar based on how thick you want the sauce to be.

Pour into a glass container and refrigerate. Be very cautious consuming sauce it is very hot.

Twisted Hot Sauce

Twisted is just how your mouth will feel when tasting this sauce. So many different tastes that your palate won't know which way to go.

Makes: 16 oz.

Prep: 10 mins

Cook: -

Ingredients:

- Red Onion (½)
- Olive Oil (4 tbsp.)
- Passion Fruit puree (2 tsp.)
- Cascabel Chile (pureed)
- Mango Purée (2 tbsp.)
- Sherry Vinegar (2 tbsp.)
- Scallions (2 stalks, chopped)
- Salt (¼ tsp.)
- Black Pepper (¼ tsp.)

Directions:

In a saucepan heat oil on med flame and sauté onion. Then add all three purees to the onion. Allow to cook for two minutes to reduce liquid.

Add vinegar and remove from flame to cool. Refrigerate to chill, take from fridge and add scallions; mix well and reheat to serve.

Mango Tango Hot Sauce

Sweet mango and kiwi pair excellently in this sauce with the pepper. Just the right amount of sweet and spicy that can be used as a glaze or otherwise, absolutely yummy.

Makes: 16 oz.

Prep: 10 mins

Cook: -

Ingredients:

- ½ doz. whole Mango (peeled)
- 7 Kiwi fruit (peeled)
- 7 Chile pepper (Habanero) steamed and seeded
- 4 Lime
- 3 Lemon
- 4 tbsp. Orange juice, frozen concentrate
- Vinegar (⅓ cup)
- Salt (1 tsp.)
- Water (2 cups)

Directions:

Firstly, wash peppers and remove the seeds then put them in a pot with water and salt. Boil on a low flame for fifteen minutes.

Drain and reserve ¾ cups of water. Put peppers with reserved water and all ingredients except vinegar into a blender; puree ingredients and pour into pot.

Turn on a medium flame and heat for ten minutes, constantly stirring.

Take pot from the flame and add vinegar and stir until it starts to cool.

Allow to cool and then put in a glass jar and refrigerate. Can last for four months and goes well with various meats.

Bajan Hot Sauce

The ingredients in this mixture combine to make a powerful burst of flavors. You can taste every bit of the Caribbean influence in every drop of this sauce.

Makes: 16 oz.

Prep: 10 mins

Cook: -

Ingredients:

- Habanero (1 doz.)
- Brown Sugar (¼ cup)
- Cayenne Peppers (2)
- Mango (sliced)
- Mustard (1 cup)
- Granulated Sugar (5 tbsp.)
- Curry Powder (1 tbsp.)
- Cumin (2 tsp.)
- Chili Powder (1 tbsp.)
- Salt (1 tsp.)
- Black Pepper (1 tsp.)

Directions:

Wash peppers and remove their stems and seeds. Then put peppers in a blender along with vinegar and grind finely.

Add all other ingredients and blend. Pour mix into glass jars and enjoy. May be refrigerated.

Quick Hot Pepper Sauce

This is a simple spicy sauce that can be made by everyone. Vinegar and salt release the spicy cayenne peppers flavor the longer it ferments. Great with fish.

Makes: 16 oz.

Prep: 10 mins

Cook: 5 mins

Ingredients:

- Distilled white vinegar (3 cups)
- 2 pounds cayenne/jalapeno pepper Seeded and chopped
- 2 tsp. Salt

Directions:

Firstly, wash peppers then remove seeds and chop. Get a large pot and put peppers, vinegar and salt and cook over a medium flame for five minutes.

Allow to cool and pour into a processor. Chop and store in a glass jar.

Can be used right away or put away to ferment in a dark place for 3 months. Strain before using.

Belizean Style Habanero Hot Sauce

Another tasty sauce using the very spicy habanero pepper, so you know you can't go wrong. Mixed spicy pepper with delectable, and it is simply goodness.

Makes: 16 oz.

Prep: 10 mins

Cook: 5 mins

Ingredients:

- Onion (chopped)
- Garlic (2 cloves, chopped)
- Oil (1 tbsp.)
- Carrots (1 cup, chopped)
- Avocado (2 cups)
- Water (2 cups)
- 3 Habanero chilies (minced)
- 3 tbsp. fresh lime juice
- Vinegar (3 tbsp.)
- Salt (1 tsp.)

Directions:

Put a pot on med flame & heat oil then add onions and sauté until they get soft. Then add water and carrots and allow to boil.

Turn the flame down to low and cook carrots till they are soft. Take pot from heat and add lime juice, chilies and salt to mixture.

Put the mixture in a food processor along with avocado and blend until smooth.

Pour into glass jars and cover. Refrigerate and use as you please.

Makes a great dip.

Jamaican Hot Sauce

Inspired by the island in the tropics made with all spices and seasonings well known on the island. The aroma of this sauce will have you "jammin."

Makes: 16 oz.

Prep: 10 mins

Cook: 5 mins

Ingredients:

- Scotch Bonnet Pepper (1 doz.)
- Indian Curry Powder (2 tsp.)
- Oil (¼ cup)
- Scallion (2 stalks)
- Onion (2)
- Salt (1 tsp.)
- Vinegar (½ cup)

Directions:

Put oil in a saucepan and heat over a medium flame. Then add curry to the oil, stirring regularly. Allow curry to cook in oil for about two minutes until curry gets dark.

Add all other ingredients except vinegar and allow to cook. Remove pan from flame and add vinegar, cover pot and allow to set. Strain into a glass jar and refrigerate. Heat again when using.

Buffalo Chipotle Hot Sauce

This can be a great sauce for Buffalo wings, ribs, or seafood. Lots of ingredients but very simple and quick to make.

Makes: 20 oz.

Prep: 10 mins

Cook: -

Ingredients:

- Dark Corn Syrup (1 ⅓ cups)
- Black Coffee (1 ⅓ cups)
- Catsup (1 cup)
- Apple Cider Vinegar (1 cup)
- Worcestershire Sauce (1 cup)
- Corn Oil (4 tbsp.)
- Chili Powder (6 tbsp.)
- Mustard (3 tbsp.)
- Salt (2 tsp.)
- Chipotle Peppers (2 tins)

Directions:

Put all ingredients into a blender and chop thoroughly.

Then put the mixture into a pot and allow to boil and thicken to your desire.

Allow to cool and enjoy. This goes well with shrimp.

Scotch Bonnet Pepper Sauce

This Scotch Bonnet recipe is another inspired by the island in the tropics. Sweet mangoes accompanied by spices and tasty 'scotchie.' Truly a keepsake, bring out the Caribbean in you with this delectable sweet sauce.

Makes: 16 oz.

Prep: 10 mins

Cook: 5 mins

Ingredients:

- Oil (1 tbsp.)
- Onions (2, diced)
- Mangoes (2, diced)
- Carrots (½ doz., diced)
- Cho cho squash (2)
- Pimento (1 doz.)
- Thyme (4 sprigs)
- Ginger (1 oz., diced)
- Sugar (½ cup)
- Scotch Bonnet peppers (1 doz.)
- Vinegar (¼ cup)

Directions:

Heat oil and cook onions till they are clear. Then add mangoes, cho cho, carrots, pimento, ginger and thyme and cook for 5 minutes.

Then add sugar and peppers, stirring occasionally. When sugar has melted add vinegar and cook for 5 minutes until carrots are soft.

Cool then pour into a blender. Puree the mix and strain. Pour into a glass jar and refrigerate. Used as desired.

Chickasaw Hot Sauce

This sauce can be used in chili or as a tasty barbecue sauce. Molasses mixed well in this dish with the pepper to give a rich aroma and flavor.

Makes: 16 oz.

Prep: 10 mins

Cook: 5 mins

Ingredients:

- Ketchup (4 cups)
- Molasses (1 ½ cups)
- Vinegar (¼ cup)
- Tabasco (2 tbsp.)
- Worcestershire Sauce (3 tbsp.)
- Lemon Juice (¼ cup)
- Onion (1 cup, diced)
- Garlic (3 cloves, chopped)
- Brown Sugar (¼ cup)
- Cayenne Pepper (1 tsp)
- Dried Mustard (3 tbsp.)
- Water (2 cups)

Directions:

Get a large saucepan and mix all ingredients together using as much or little water to create a creamy mix.

Place saucepan over medium heat and allow to boil, stir regularly to avoid sticking.

Lower the heat and simmer for about 30 minutes. Add water if mixture gets too thick.

Remove from heat and pour in mason jars. May be used in chili or as a barbecue sauce.

Chiltepin Hot Sauce

Chiltepin is otherwise known as bird peppers, tepin, and bird's eye.

Makes: 16 oz.

Prep: 10 mins

Cook: 5 mins

Ingredients:

- Chiltepins (2 cups)
- Garlic (8 cloves)
- Salt (1 tsp.)
- Oregano (1 tsp.)
- Coriander Seed (1 tsp.)
- Water (1 cup)
- Apple Cider Vinegar (1 tsp.)

Directions:

Blend all ingredients thoroughly until smooth for three to four minutes.

Pour into a clean glass jar and refrigerate for a day. Keep refrigerated until it needs to be used.

Conclusion

Well, there you have it! Tangy and delicious hot sauce recipes for you to try out at home. Be sure to try out all of the recipes in this book, because you never know which one might end up being your favorite! Also, if you love these recipes, make sure to share them with your friends and family!

About the Author

A native of Indianapolis, Indiana, Valeria Ray found her passion for cooking while she was studying English Literature at Oakland City University. She decided to try a cooking course with her friends and the experience changed her forever. She enrolled at the Art Institute of Indiana which offered extensive courses in the culinary Arts. Once Ray dipped her toe in the cooking world, she never looked back.

When Valeria graduated, she worked in French restaurants in the Indianapolis area until she became the head chef at one of the 5-star establishments in the area. Valeria's attention to taste and visual detail caught the eye of a local business person who expressed an interest in publishing her recipes. Valeria began her secondary career authoring cookbooks and e-books which she tackled with as much talent and gusto as her first career. Her passion for food leaps off the page of her books which have colourful anecdotes and stunning pictures of dishes she has prepared herself.

Valeria Ray lives in Indianapolis with her husband of 15 years, Tom, her daughter, Isobel and their loveable Golden Retriever, Goldy. Valeria enjoys cooking special dishes in her large, comfortable kitchen where the family gets involved in preparing meals. This successful, dynamic chef is an inspiration to culinary students and novice cooks everywhere.

Author's Afterthoughts

Thank you for Purchasing my book and taking the time to read it from front to back. I am always grateful when a reader chooses my work and I hope you enjoyed it!

With the vast selection available online, I am touched that you chose to be purchasing my work and take valuable time out of your life to read it. My hope is that you feel you made the right decision.

I very much would like to know what you thought of the book. Please take the time to write an honest and informative review on Amazon.com. Your experience and opinions will be of great benefit to me and those readers looking to make an informed choice.

With much thanks,

Valeria Ray

Made in the USA
Las Vegas, NV
07 November 2023